AT HOME IN WORLD WAR TWO

EVACUATION

Stewart Ross

Evans Brothers Limited

LEAVE THIS TO US
SONNY — <u>YOU</u> OUGHT
TO BE OUT OF LONDON

MINISTRY OF HEALTH EVACUATION SCHEME

Published by Evans Brothers Limited
2A Portman Mansions
Chiltern Street
London W1U 6NR

© 2002 White-Thomson Publishing Limited

Produced for Evans Brothers Limited by
White-Thomson Publishing Ltd
2/3 St Andrew's Place
Lewes, East Sussex BN7 1UP

Printed in Dubai

Editor: Philippa Smith
Consultant: Terry Charman, Historian, Research and Information Department,
Imperial War Museum
Designer: Christopher Halls, Mind's Eye Design, Lewes
Proofreader: Alison Cooper

British Library Cataloguing in Publication Data
Ross, Stewart
    Evacuation. - (At home in World War Two)
    1. World War, 1939-1945 - Evacuation of civilians - Great Britain
    2. World War, 1939-1945 - Children
    I. Title
    941'.084
ISBN: 0 237 52306 X

Captions:
Cover and this page: A Government propaganda poster aimed at mothers. It suggests
that all children should be evacuated away from the dangers of air raids in London to
the safety of the countryside.
Cover (centre): A boy from Battersea, evacuated to a farm, helps with the harvest.
Cover (background): A teacher leads pupils from the bomb-damaged Old Woolwich
Road School, London. They are all wearing gas masks in case there is poison gas in
the air.
Title page: The great evacuation from London. Schoolchildren on a platform at
Paddington Station about to set off for the west of England, and safety.
Contents page: A group of city children, evacuated to Devon, enjoying the new
experience of life in the countryside.

For sources of quoted material see page 31.

CONTENTS

SAVE THE CHILDREN!

Britain joined World War Two in September 1939 when it declared war on Germany. France, Belgium, the Netherlands, Poland and other countries fought with Britain against Germany and, later, against Italy. In 1941, the USSR and the USA joined the war on the same side as Britain. Japan joined the side of Germany and Italy. By this time the fighting had spread right round the world. The war finally ended in 1945.

The fighting in World War Two took place on land, at sea and in the air. Although aircraft had been used previously in World War One (1914–18), this was the first big war in which aircraft played such an important part. Bomber planes dropped thousands of tonnes of bombs on towns and cities. Some places were completely flattened. Air raids destroyed millions of homes and many thousands of people were killed and injured.

▲ *Newspaper placards tell of the German invasion of Poland, 1 September 1939. The evacuation of children (and many of their mothers) began immediately and was complete by the time Britain went to war on 3 September.*

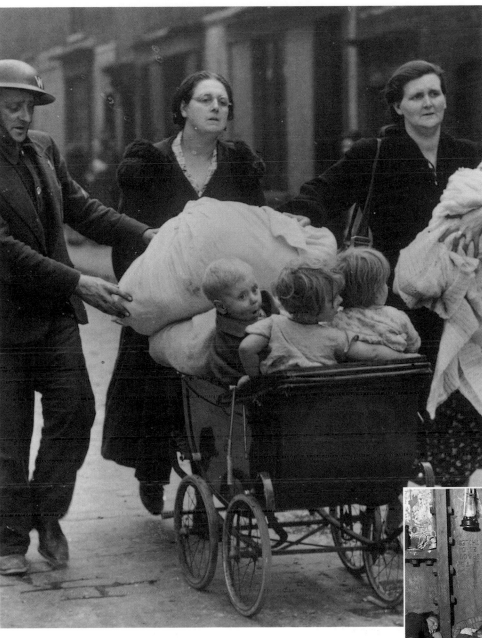

Adolf Hitler became leader of Germany in 1933. Backed by his Nazi Party, he removed those who were against him and began taking over neighbouring countries. After Germany took over Czechoslovakia, Britain and France promised other countries that they would oppose Nazi aggression if the Germans attacked anyone else. On 1 September 1939, Hitler invaded Poland. Two days later, Britain and France declared war on Germany.

◀ *An air-raid warden helps mothers and their babies, bombed out of their east London homes, to find shelter somewhere safe.*

Because of air raids, no one could escape the war. Everyone's home might be in the 'front line'. That is why we say the war was fought on the 'Home Front' as well as the battle front.

Fighter planes and special anti-aircraft guns tried to shoot the bombers down. But this was very difficult at night when the bombers could not be seen. Experts said the bombers would 'always get through', making city life very dangerous. There were two ways of protecting people from air raids. First, they could take cover in strong bomb shelters. Second, they could move away from the places likely to be bombed. This was known as 'evacuation' and is the subject of this book.

▲ *Evacuation was not compulsory. These parents, sheltering overnight in Liverpool Street underground station, London, had decided to keep their daughter (and her doll) with them, despite the danger from air raids.*

INTO THE UNKNOWN

All kinds of people were evacuated – pregnant mothers, mothers with small children, the sick and the elderly. By far the largest group, however, were schoolchildren. George Clarke, a Londoner, watched mothers and children gathering at a meeting place in Bethnal Green, London.

'The feeling amongst the mothers was generally quite calm. Of course, many were upset at parting with their children – many were crying and hugging their children.

But the children's behaviour was quite different. Some remained very quiet. They held tightly on to their mums' hands, not really knowing what was going on. Others were quite happy, especially when the time came for them to part from their mothers. This seemed extraordinary. Oh, there were a few that burst into tears and cried, "I want my mummy". But in general the children seemed to feel much better when they were left amongst themselves.'

▲ *Mothers and their young children gather at London's Victoria Station ready for evacuation to an unknown destination in the countryside. You can see a steam train in the background.*

These London children were waiting to be taken by train to the safety of the countryside. The 1930s had been a tough time for working-class British families and most of them had not been able to afford holidays away from home. For the majority of children who had not travelled outside London before, evacuation was an adventure.

▶ *Children were allowed to take with them only what they could carry. This little boy needed both hands to carry his heavy suitcase.*

Not all partings were well ordered, and not all evacuation was by train, as Leonard Smith, then aged 13, recalled:

'We marched from the school with all the mums and children crying and carrying on. We went aboard the Golden Eagle at West Street Pier in Gravesend, and just before the Golden Eagle sailed the town band played "Auld Lang Syne".'

The *Golden Eagle* took evacuees down the Kent coast, away from London.

'No children will be taken without their parents' consent. That consent will be held to be given if parents send their children to school on a day announced for evacuation.'

Government announcement, 1939

Often, even the people in charge of groups of evacuees did not know exactly where they were going. No wonder many of the children were excited – for them it was a journey into the unknown.

GOVERNMENT EVACUATION SCHEME

The Government have ordered evacuation of registered school children.

If your children are registered, visit their assembly point at once and read the instructions on the notice board.

The name and address of the assembly point is given on the notice to parents.

Posters notifying arrival will be displayed at the schools at which the children assemble for evacuation.

The County Hall, S.E.1

E. M. RICH, Education Officer

▲ *Well-made plans. Parents registered their children for evacuation before war broke out. When the evacuation plan was put into operation, notices like these told parents what to do.*

◀ *The boy from the East End of London in the centre of the picture was clearly enjoying his evacuation on 2 September 1939. War was declared the next day.*

SAFETY FIRST

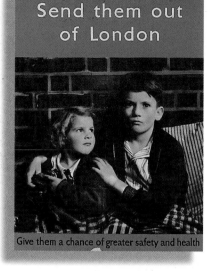

MOTHERS Send them out of London

Give them a chance of greater safety and health

▲ *This government poster urged women to register their children for evacuation.*

Evacuation began on 1 September 1939, two days before Britain went to war. Experts said enemy bombers would kill 10,000 people every day. The Government wanted children out of the way before the attacks started.

Evacuation was voluntary. The Government expected 3.5 million people to leave for the safety of the countryside. In fact, only about 1.5 million did and, of these, 735,000 were children travelling alone.

The *Daily Mirror*, keen to support the Government's evacuation scheme, tried to reassure mothers who stayed behind:

'You have done a brave and self-sacrificing thing in sending your children away from the danger areas.'
4 September 1939

When the bombing did not start in 1939, people wondered what all the fuss had been about. They said they were in a 'phoney war'. By March 1940 1.2 million mothers and children had returned home. Then, in the summer of 1940, the Germans conquered France and prepared to invade Britain. Months of almost non-stop bombing began in July.

'We were assailed on all sides with propaganda to persuade parents to send their children to safety.'

A mother from Stirling, Scotland

TAKE THEM BACK! TAKE THEM BACK! TAKE THEM BACK!..

DON'T do it, mother—

LEAVE THE CHILDREN WHERE THEY ARE

ISSUED BY THE MINISTRY OF HEALTH

◀ *Britain experienced few air raids during the early months of the war. Believing the bombers would never come in large numbers, many evacuated mothers and children returned home. The Government feared otherwise, as this poster shows. The ghostly figure urging the mother to go home is Adolf Hitler, the leader of Nazi Germany.*

A second evacuation was organised in June 1940. This time about 620,000 children left the cities. They were also moved from the south-east of England, where the German armies were planning to land. A third, smaller evacuation took place in 1944, when only children from London and the southern counties were evacuated (see page 24).

Sometimes whole schools, including teachers, were evacuated. This happened to many nursery schools and private schools. The King's School, Canterbury, for example, moved to a hotel in Cornwall. Some schools joined up with others in safe areas, but normally just a class or a family were evacuated together.

Individual families also arranged their own evacuations. Two million mothers and children went to stay with families and friends in the country. Many stayed there until after the war was over.

▲ The children who remained behind in the cities soon became used to the dangers of air raids. This boy is repairing his cart close to an unexploded bomb.

◀ Have we done the right thing? Parents did their best to appear cheerful as they waved goodbye to their children.

As well as schools and hospitals, many Government offices were evacuated out of London. Edna Miller, whose husband was a civil servant based in London, remembered:

'Jim came home one evening and said, "Get packing, Edna. We're off to north Wales." I thought he had arranged a holiday at first. Then he explained about his office being evacuated and off we went. Actually, it was like a holiday, really.'

9

BAGS AND BAGGAGE

Before the outbreak of war the Government issued a list of what each child should take with them if they were evacuated. First, they had to have their gas mask. It was meant to be carried in its case so it could be put on quickly.

Gas masks were needed in case bombs containing poison gas were dropped. Poison gas had been used against soldiers in World War One, causing horrible injuries. Although it was never used in air raids in World War Two, everyone was given a gas mask which they had to carry all the time, just in case.

'We were threatened with death if we lost our gas masks.'

Nicola Harrison, a young child living near Bromley, Kent

▲ A young child in a gas mask. The masks were smelly and frightening to wear. Children were issued with 'Mickey Mouse' masks – coloured orange and blue – to make them more attractive.

Each child was supposed to pack two sets of underwear, spare shoes and socks or stockings, a warm coat, a sweater, handkerchiefs and pyjamas or a night-dress. They were also told to take soap, a towel, a toothbrush, toothpaste and a hairbrush and comb.

Hitler will send no warning – so always carry your gas mask

ISSUED BY THE MINISTRY OF HOME SECURITY

◄ A Government poster reminds everyone to carry their gas mask. Although gas was not used during World War Two, there was always a fear that it might be.

▶ Children from St Michael's School, Chelsea, their precious possessions carefully parcelled and tied up with string, gather for evacuation in September 1939. Each child carried a square box containing a gas mask.

This list of things to pack was drawn up by people who did not know how poor some families were. Many children did not own a coat, for example. Their parents certainly could not afford a spare pair of shoes. And lots of children had never even seen a toothbrush.

Children had to take another bag with enough food to last them for a day. They were meant to carry their own possessions but teachers had to help the younger ones. Finally, each child had a large label with their name on it attached to the front of their clothes. This made it easier to send them to the right place, and stop them getting lost on the way.

Barbara Letchford, who went to stay with Mrs Hall in the Kent countryside in 1939, never forgot the packet of sandwiches her mother had prepared for her:

'. . . that first evening I sat at the dining room table with these sandwiches and Mrs Hall asked me if I was worried about something. I said I didn't know how long the sandwiches were to last so I didn't know how many to eat this evening.'

After much heart searching, Beryl Cooper from South London decided she could not face being apart from her children:

'. . . all of a sudden I thought no, I won't let them go. I cannot be separated from them. I rushed down the stairs and met my husband and I sent him to go and get them. He just took them straight out of the line and brought them back with their big tickets on.'

▲ The label tied to Betty Minchin when she was evacuated from Lowestoft Secondary School, on the east coast of England, to Worksop in Nottinghamshire on 2 June 1940. Children were evacuated from east coast ports in case of bombing, an invasion or (as had happened during World War One) bombardment from enemy ships.

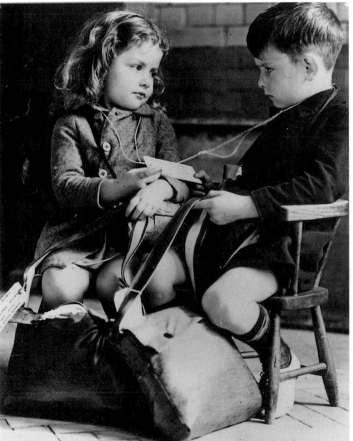

▶ June Bryant shows her evacuation label to her brother Tony as they wait to be evacuated from Clerkenwell Station, London, on 9 June 1940.

ALL ABOARD!

When the bombing in London became really heavy, Eileen Roberts' mother decided to send her baby daughter to safety. Eileen recalls her mother's memories of this:

'Mum had to arrive at Waterloo Station on a particular date, at a particular time. She turned up at the appointed time and was met by a woman who introduced herself as a representative of the Government authority. She asked my mother if her child was Eileen.

When my mother answered "Yes", the woman took me from Mum's arms, walked away with me, and got on the train that was standing at the platform. My mother didn't know the woman's name, or where I was being taken. She watched the train leaving the station without knowing where I had gone.

For a whole week Mum had no idea what had happened to me! Can you imagine that?'

▼ *A steam train of the type that carried many evacuees away from cities to the safety of the countryside.*

Evacuees were normally older than baby Eileen. They were evacuated mostly by train. Others went by bus, car or, occasionally, by boat. The teachers who travelled with their classes acted as mothers and fathers. They comforted the children, made sure they had enough to eat and drink and organised queues at the toilets.

► *Policemen supervise a group of evacuees setting off for their new homes by bus.*

Most important, on rail journeys they had to make sure each child got off at the right station. Some journeys took all day. The steam trains puffed slowly through the countryside, stopping at station after station. By the time they arrived, the children were usually bewildered and exhausted.

'Now be a good boy and come and look at the engine . . .'

A woman trying to comfort her son, who was about to be evacuated.

'Mum, ain't you coming too?'

A question heard at countless evacuation centres throughout London.

'I remember . . . arriving at a railway station, God knows which one it was, and then arriving, after what seemed to me such a long journey, in a place called Bury. That journey was just for ever.'

Nicola Harrison

▲ *I don't want to go! Surrounded by luggage, this small girl from Chatham in Kent was clearly distressed by the whole evacuation experience.*

◀ *As the evacuation train puffs out of the station, anxious children wave goodbye to their mothers.*

DESTINATION UNKNOWN

▼ *Places from which most children were evacuated and the areas to which large numbers were sent.*

The aim of evacuation was to get people out of danger. The Government listed nine areas to be evacuated. These were big cities and ports, including London, Manchester, Liverpool and Southampton.

Some cities, such as Glasgow and Belfast, were not evacuated. The Government believed enemy bombers would not be able to fly that far. But they were wrong. Glasgow and Belfast were both heavily bombed and many people died, including children.

Evacuees went to country areas where no bombs fell. They stayed in small towns, villages and farmhouses in the countryside. Lancashire, Sussex and Yorkshire took the most. Some children from London ended up hundreds of kilometres from home. A few even went abroad (see page 26).

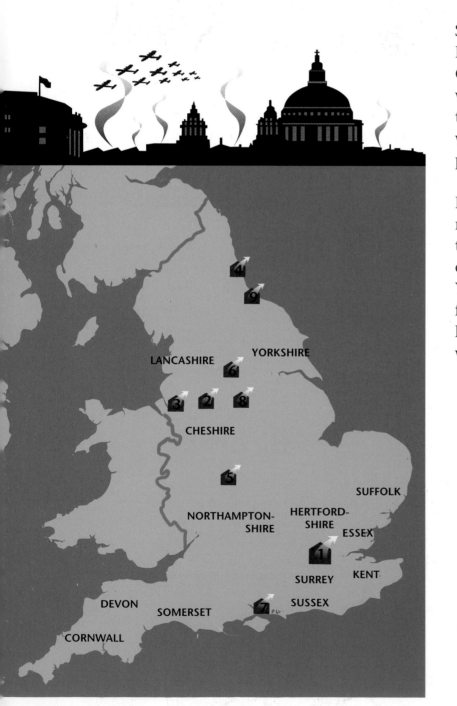

PLACES FROM WHICH MOST CHILDREN WERE EVACUATED:

1	London	241,000
2	Manchester/Salford	84,343
3	Merseyside	79,930
4	Newcastle/Sunderland	52,494
5	Birmingham/West Midlands	32,688
6	Leeds/Bradford	26,419
7	Portsmouth/Southampton	23,145
8	Sheffield/East Midlands	13,871
9	Teeside	8,052

AREAS TO WHICH LARGE NUMBERS OF CHILDREN WERE SENT:

Lancashire	Northamptonshire
Sussex	Hertfordshire
Yorkshire	Suffolk
Kent	Somerset
Cheshire	Surrey
Essex	

The first evacuation was a remarkable operation. In three days hundreds of thousands of people, mostly young children, were moved all over the country. At the same time, soldiers, sailors and airmen were also on the move, getting ready for the outbreak of war. Amazingly, not one child was lost or injured.

Imagine what evacuation day was like for inner-city children. In the morning they woke up amid familiar objects and faces. After saying goodbye to their mothers, they were lined up, listed and sent on a long and tiring journey. That night they went to bed in a strange house surrounded by the unfamiliar sounds of the countryside. It was an experience they remembered for the rest of their lives.

▲ *Smashed shops and offices in St Anne's Square, Manchester, after an air raid just before Christmas, 1940. Manchester was one of the large British cities targeted by German bombers.*

▼ *On her first morning in her new home, an evacuee helps her foster mother feed the chickens.*

15

SOMEWHERE SAFE

It might be YOU!

CARING FOR EVACUEES
IS A NATIONAL SERVICE

ISSUED BY THE MINISTRY OF HEALTH

▲ *Not everyone was keen to take in evacuees. This Government poster reminded country-dwellers of their duty to help with the war effort by taking in the homeless from the cities.*

While the children were travelling to their destinations, they were told only that they were going 'somewhere safe'. Even when they finally arrived, and were told where they were, they were still confused. The name of a country town or village meant nothing to children who had never been out of their home city. Even county names did not mean much to them. All they knew of 'Somerset' or 'Surrey' was that they were cricket teams.

Where possible, whole classes or schools were kept together. One nursery school was sent to a huge country mansion. The building was approached through a stone arch that stood at the end of a very long drive. When the school bus reached the arch, the driver found it was too low to drive under. Everyone had to get out and carry their bags up the drive to the house.

▶ *A group of evacuees arriving at Dartington Hall in Devon. Inner-city children would never have seen such a magnificent mansion before.*

Normally, children stayed in twos or threes in ordinary houses. When they got off the train or bus, they were led off to their new homes. Teachers took some of them. Others were taken by the local policeman or the 'billeting officer'.

Sometimes children were led to the village hall or vicarage. Here they met up with their foster parents. Where no plans had been made, the children stood about while adults chose whom they wanted. Happily, this sort of horrible experience was rare.

Sixteen London evacuees arrived at Lilian Parkes' house in Seal, Kent, without warning:

> 'There was a knock on the door of this big house and I opened the door and there was the billeting officer pushing all these children into the hall.'

Anita Bowers, from a West Indian family living in West Ham, London, found the process of being chosen very distressing:

> 'We were the last to be picked. You couldn't blame them, they didn't have any coloured people there in those days. I stood with my little brother Richard, Mum and the baby. I think we stood there all morning.'

'There's room in my heart for a hundred children, and I'd squeeze them all into my house, too, if I could.'

A Scotswoman prepared to accept evacuees, *Daily Mirror*, 4 September 1939

▲ Joseph Hill, a billeting officer responsible for the evacuees in his area, calls on Mrs Holdsworth to see that she and the three London children staying with her are all right.

◀ Joseph Hill explains to Mrs Holdsworth how she can claim money for the upkeep of the children who are staying with her.

'MY OWN TOWEL'

For many inner-city children, moving to a large house in the country was like entering a different world. Ron Collins, who had always used a public bath house before, recalled the house he went to.

'I remember it was so different from our house in Stepney, London. There were two of us who had been evacuated to this house in the Chiltern Hills.

The house had a bathroom and an indoor lavatory upstairs. It was wonderful having my own towel hanging on the door, and all the toiletries were on the side next to the wash basin that even had hot water.

A long white bath was to one side which also had hot and cold water that you could control while sitting in the bath. It was quite different from the council baths, where the hot and cold controls were outside, and you had to call out to the attendant that you wanted either more hot, or more cold water.

I think the only thing I didn't like was that I had to bath three times a week instead of only once, but we soon got used to it and enjoyed it.'

▼ The homes they left behind – a terrace of London houses after an air raid. Evacuees were startled at the contrast between crowded houses like these and the airy country cottages, farmhouses and mansions that were their new homes.

Ron's memories may seem strange. They make sense only if we remember that in 1940 the homes of most working-class families had no bathroom and only an outside toilet. Hot running water was a luxury, too. One child upset her foster parents by crying and refusing to get into the bath tub. 'My Mum said I'd die if I went in one of them!' she explained.

Unusually, Nicola Harrison found the conditions in the home she was evacuated to worse than those at home:

'I don't think I had a bath the whole time I was there. And I don't remember having my hair washed once.'

Getting changed for bed was another thing children found strange. Lots of working-class children slept in their shirts and underclothes. They had never worn pyjamas or a night-dress before. Nor were they used to clean sheets on their own bed – at home most of them shared a bed with their brothers and sisters.

'One family . . . wouldn't sleep on a bed, they'd never slept on a bed before so they refused to get into it.'

Lilian Parkes

A woman explained why she wanted to take in evacuees in 1939:

'What are a few finger-marks on the paint beside saving these poor kiddies from the horror of war?'

Daily Mirror, 4 September 1939

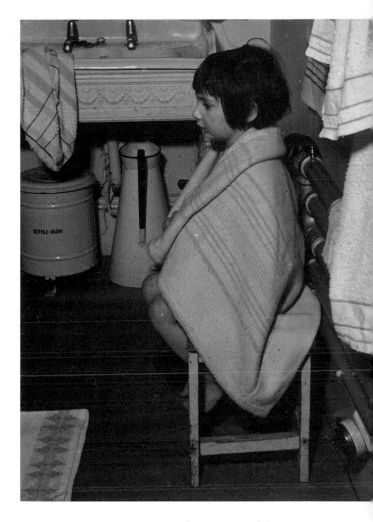

▲ Bath time. For many evacuees from poor families bathrooms and hot and cold running water were luxuries they had not met before. Their new foster parents, on the other hand, were frequently shocked by how dirty the children were.

▶ Small children, evacuated from a London nursery school, asleep in their cots in a big country house. Their few belongings are in baskets underneath the cots.

NEW FAMILIES

Evacuation brought together very different people. The hosts of evacuees were quite often middle-class, middle-aged couples with quite large houses. The evacuees, as we have seen, were mostly working-class children from the poorest parts of large cities.

The children took a while to get used to their new homes. Some children did not settle and soon returned home. Many others were very happy and stayed with their foster parents for the whole war. When they were old enough, they went to work on local farms.

A number of foster parents were shocked by the children they cared for. They found them dirty, bad-mannered and sickly. Many city children had nits and skin diseases. Their hosts were afraid of catching the children's diseases and did not treat them kindly.

▲ *A new family. Anne Norris at tea-time with the six children she has taken into her country home.*

► *Evacuees who went to live with Mrs Cluton (standing and serving lunch) were amazed at the luxury of her meal times. Mrs Carter and her two evacuee children, Michael and Angela (sitting either side of her), are enjoying her delicious food.*

Evacuees kept in touch with their family and friends by letter and occasional visits. However, some mothers almost never wrote to their children. They seemed pleased to have them out of the way. Lizzie Graham was told that her mother had been killed in an air raid in 1940. But when she returned home after the war, she found her mum alive and well!

'. . . to be taken away from your home and family, as you can imagine, is so very hard for a child. For many evacuees it was to scar them for life – you must remember that not all were cared for as well as Mrs Smith cared for us.'

Pam Hattersley, who was evacuated from London to a village near Colchester, Essex

▲ A special cheap-day return train ticket issued to parents wishing to visit members of their family who had been evacuated. The ticket is 'third class' – in those days first, second and third class tickets were available.

◀ Mrs Carter arrives at the farm where her two children, Michael and Angela, have been evacuated.

'In the main they were really homesick, both the mothers and the children.'

Ken Gerring, who worked for the council in Ashford, Kent, after visiting evacuees from his home town who had been sent to Oxfordshire

SCHOOL IN WARTIME

Children's education suffered because of evacuation. Pupils did best when a whole school was moved together. By 1943, 47,000 country mansions had been turned into schools or hostels. Even so, things were not easy. One school held its assemblies in a garage. Another used the local pub as a classroom.

Many young teachers joined the armed forces or moved to other war work. This put an extra strain on those who were left, who were often quite elderly. When they were evacuated with their class, they had to be mum, dad and teacher all in one. Classwork was difficult, too, because books, pencils and paper were in short supply.

▲ *London children who have been evacuated to Wales being taught some useful words of Welsh.*

After they had settled down in the country, evacuees went to the local school. Most of these schools were very small. Where there was not enough room for the new arrivals, the school day was divided in two. Some pupils went in the morning, others in the afternoon. This made every day a half-holiday.

▼ *Classes in the sunshine. Evacuee children being taught in the corner of a field where a farmer is cutting hay with a horse-drawn mower.*

Dolly Bliss, whose own children had grown up and left home, worked with children evacuated from the slums of Liverpool. She was surprised they did not share her love of the countryside.

> 'I showed them cows – they quaked with fear. I took them for walks in the hills – they did nothing but puff and pant and complain. All the time they said they were bored. It was hopeless!'

City children's reaction to the countryside was sometimes quite surprising:

> 'They call this spring, Mum, and they have one down here every year.'

An evacuee's letter home

▼ City girls gather spring primroses from the hedgerows. Most evacuees treasured their countryside experiences long after they had returned home.

A nursery school teacher working with very young children evacuated from London to a country house in Hertfordshire remembered how they used to play:

> '. . . if you peeped through the nursery door during "rest period", you would find the cots "blacked out" with blankets, and the children playing "shelters"; but a sudden clap of thunder would cause a stampede for the stairs! All under five, many born since the beginning of the war, "blitz" babies knew instinctively that the ground floor was the safest.'

▼ School closed. Parents and pupils examine bomb damage at Moorside Road School, south-east London, the morning after an air raid.

After evacuation, many inner-city schools were used as emergency canteens or centres for the homeless. When pupils returned, as many did in 1939–40, they found they could not use their old school buildings.

Later, a large number of city schools were destroyed by enemy bombs. Youth crime increased as pupils hung about the streets all day. But considering the difficult wartime conditions, it is surprising just how well educated wartime children were.

DOODLEBUG!

The last evacuation took place in 1944 when, in June, the Germans began firing V1 missiles at London. Known as 'doodlebugs' or 'buzz bombs', V1s were really pilotless planes. They were not very accurate, as William Mack remembers.

'Because I was a dentist I wasn't called up. We lived in Sevenoaks in Kent but I worked in London.

Yes, I remember some children from Bermondsey were evacuated to our town. Scruffy bunch they were! The last lot came in 1944. That was during the doodlebug attacks.

I remember thinking at the time how silly it was to move them to Kent because the doodlebugs flew right over us. "Doodlebug Alley" they called it. They were aimed at London, but you never knew when they were going to come down. Lots fell short.

One minute they'd be buzzing along. Then the engine would stop and wallop! There goes a cow shed or a pub or whatever. It wasn't very safe anywhere, but I suppose the kids were better off out of London.'

▲ Life in a wartime city. A family welcomes neighbours from the bombed-out house on the opposite side of the street to share a meal with them. Children who remained in the cities faced constant danger from enemy bombs.

▲ A German V1 'flying bomb'. V1s were also nicknamed 'doodlebugs' or 'buzz bombs' because of the buzzing noise made by their engines.

◀ This injured Londoner, being carried on a stretcher, was a victim of a German 'doodlebug' flying bomb in June, 1944. By March 1945, around 5,000 of these V1s had reached Britain.

The *Evening News*, 6 July 1944, reacted strongly to the V1 attacks on London:

> 'We welcome the news that children and mothers are being encouraged to leave, and that deep shelters are to be opened. Both these decisions, in our view, should have been made earlier . . . London is no place for children.'

From September 1944, the Germans fired V2 missiles. These were 12-metre rockets with a one-tonne warhead. They were particularly terrifying because they could not be shot down and landed without warning, causing enormous damage.

One of the two 'doodlebug evacuees' taken in by May Lawton, a teacher and ambulance driver, was quite a handful:

> 'I had a lot of trouble with [him] – pinching apples, running round the garden at teatime in his socks. So I made him wash his own socks once and he told his mother. I had quite a row with her about it.'

▲ Places in London's deep shelters (far enough underground to be safe from the massive blast of a V1 flying bomb) were reserved for ticket holders. These were mostly women and children. The V1 attacks of 1944 set off a third wave of evacuation from the capital.

◄ A father sits down to breakfast on his own. There is a letter from his wife on the table and a photograph of him with his family on the sideboard. Evacuation was often just as painful for those left behind as for the evacuees.

OVERSEAS

When it seemed certain that war would break out, it was suggested that children might be evacuated abroad. At first the Government did not like the idea. It was expensive and gave the impression that Britain was expecting to be defeated.

Some wealthier families, who could afford their own fares, did go abroad. By the spring of 1940, over 10,000 mothers and children had left for safer homes overseas, 5,000 of these to the USA.

When it looked as if the Germans were going to invade Britain, the Government changed its mind. It set up the Children's Overseas Reception Board (CORB) to organise the evacuation of children to Australia, New Zealand, South Africa and Canada.

◀ British children boarding a steamer that will take them to Australia. Although Australia was beyond the reach of the Nazis, in 1942 there was a real possibility that it would be invaded by Japan.

▼ The tragic sinking of the City of Benares made headlines all around the world.

'CARRY ON' CALL BY BEAVERBROOK:

Daily Sketch

U-Boat Leaves 83 British Evacuees to Drown in Storm

NAZIS TORPEDO MERCY SHIP, KILL CHILDREN
M.P. and Nurses Among Missing

In two weeks CORB received 200,000 applications for overseas evacuation. The board could not cope and refused to take any more requests. Between July and September 1940 it arranged for about 2,644 children to leave Britain. Most, but not all, arrived safely.

On 30 August 1940 the Dutch liner *Volendam*, with 320 British evacuee children on board, was sunk by a German submarine. The children managed to get into the lifeboats and were saved.

Another group, in the *City of Benares*, was not so lucky. Like the *Volendam*, the *City of Benares* was bound for Canada. On board were 90 British evacuee children. On the stormy night of 17 September 1940 it was hit by a German torpedo and sank. Only 13 children of the CORB survived. When the terrible news reached Britain, the Government stopped official overseas evacuation.

▲ British evacuees on board the liner *Samaria* wave a greeting as they steam into New York harbour after safely crossing the Atlantic, 14 October 1940.

'The vessel [City of Benares] was attacked at night, and gallant rescue efforts were largely defeated by tempestuous weather, many boats being swamped in the heavy sea. Women and children endured severe hardships with conspicuous courage.'

'A warship which proceeded to the scene of the disaster has brought into a northern port the following children: – Rex Ernest Thorne, aged 13, of 10, Derwent Gardens, Wembley (sister dead); Jack Sidney Keeley, 8, of 138, Cowley Road, Brixton (sister dead); John Baker, 7, of 90, Townead Road, Southall (brother dead).'

Both quotes taken from The *Times*, 23 September 1940

Mary Cornish, one of the women travelling with the children, managed to get her charges into a lifeboat:

'With some canvas the seamen rigged up a shelter in the bows and we lay there protected in some measure from the wild seas, but we had only one blanket for three boys. Our main trouble was to keep our circulation at least partially going.'

Toronto Globe and Mail, 27 September 1940

WAS IT ALL WORTH IT?

Historians and social workers disagree about the evacuation of children. Those who say it was not worth it point out:

1. Between September 1939 and March 1940 evacuation cost about £9 million. The money could have been better spent on warships and fighter planes.
2. Evacuation was unnecessary as bomb damage was not as bad as expected. Instead of 10,000 deaths from each raid, air raids killed 60,595 people in the whole war. Most children would have been safe at home if they had gone to an air-raid shelter during an attack.
3. Evacuation caused a great deal of unhappiness. Families were broken up and parents and children made miserable.
4. Children's education was severely disrupted.

'I'm blowed if I'd let my kids go again!'

A woman whose children were evacuated in September 1939 and had returned home by the end of the year.

▶ *The pain of separation. The splitting up of families caused much heartache. Even today people disagree about whether wartime evacuation was really the right course of action.*

Supporters of evacuation argue:

1. Evacuation did save lives. If the millions of children had remained in the cities, many of them would certainly have been killed.
2. Evacuation showed that the Government cared. It gave poor parents a chance to send their children to safety. This helped keep up people's spirits.
3. Many children enjoyed evacuation. It was an exciting adventure.
4. Evacuation brought the nation together. It gave children from the cities a chance of a better life. At the same time, it taught wealthier families just how tough life was for the poor people of Britain's slums. After the war, the Government made a real effort to get rid of bad housing and see that everyone got a decent wage.

▲ Happy to be out of danger, a pair of evacuee boys feed the pigs on the farm to which they were sent.

No two evacuation experiences were same, as these two comments show:

'I hated this old couple I was with and they hated me. Mum came and took me home after only two weeks.'

Anne Grant, who was evacuated from Birmingham to Warwickshire

'No, I wasn't homesick. A bit bored sometimes. But looking back it was one of the best times of my life.'

George Willis, who was evacuated from London to Buckinghamshire

◀ Home at last! A group of British children, evacuated to Australia at the beginning of the war, seem delighted to be back home again five years later. The photograph was taken on the deck of HMS Andes in Southampton, September 1945.

GLOSSARY

air-raid shelter A place where people could shelter from a bomb attack. Many were underground. They were usually made of steel or concrete.

anti-aircraft gun A gun for shooting at planes.

armed forces The army, navy and air force.

billeting officer The person who decided where evacuees were to stay in a country town or village.

blacked out During the war all windows had to be covered so no light showed outside at night. This was called the black-out. It was done to make it harder for enemy bombers to find target towns in the darkness.

Blitz The heavy bombing of a city. 'Blitz' comes from the German word *Blitzkrieg* which means 'lightning war'.

canteen A place where food and drink is served.

consent Agreement.

evacuee Someone who was evacuated.

foster parents Couples who look after a child when their real parents ('birth parents') are unable to do so. The people who took in evacuee children were foster parents.

gas mask A mask that fits over the mouth and nose. It filters out poisonous gas in the air.

invaded Moved into another country by force. In 1940 the Germans invaded France and planned to invade Britain.

Nazi Party Germany's National Socialist Party. It was led by Adolf Hitler and followed his ideas and wishes.

slum A house that is not fit for people to live in.

vicarage A vicar's house. A vicar is a priest of the Church of England.

voluntary Something one can choose to do – or not.

PROJECTS ON EVACUATION

Write an illustrated diary of an evacuee, using as much primary evidence as you can.

Were people evacuated to or from the area where you live? If they were, try to find out more about them.

A project on evacuation needs information from *primary* and *secondary* sources. Secondary sources, mainly books and websites, are listed on the next page. They give mostly other people's views about evacuation. Primary sources come from the time of the evacuation itself, like some of the quotations in this book. They make a project really interesting and original.

Here are some ways of getting hold of primary information:
* Talking to people who were evacuated or who lived in areas that evacuees went to.
* Looking for objects remaining from the time of the evacuation. These can be large things like buildings. For example, is there an air-raid shelter still standing near you? Smaller objects include steel helmets and gas masks.
* Visiting museums. Most local museums have excellent displays about their area during World War Two. National museums, like the Imperial War Museum in London, have a great deal of information.
* Looking at old photographs in family albums.
* Reading printed memories. There are many collections of old photographs, too. Ask at your local library what there is for your area.
* Visiting websites that contain primary information – but read the warning on the next page first!

FURTHER INFORMATION

BOOKS TO READ

Britain Through the Ages: Britain Since 1930, Stewart Ross (Evans, 1995)
Children of the Blitz, Robert Westall (Macmillan, 1995)
Coming Alive: Dear Mum, I Miss You! Stewart Ross (Evans, 2001)
Coming Alive: What If the Bomb Goes Off? Stewart Ross (Evans, 2001)
The Evacuation, Martin Parsons, Penny Starns and Charles Wheeler (DSM, 1999)
Family Life: Second World War, Nigel Smith (Hodder Wayland, 1998)
The History Detective Investigates Britain at War: Evacuation, Martin Parsons (Hodder Wayland, 2000)
History in Writing: The Second World War, Christine Hatt (Evans, 2000)
In Grandma's Day, Faye Gardner (Evans, 2000)
Investigating the Home Front, Alison Honey (The National Trust, 1996)
Memories of Childhood (The classic stories of **War Boy** and **After the War Was Over**), Michael Foreman (Pavilion, 2000)
On the Trail of World War II in Britain, Alex Stewart (Watts, 1999)

WEBSITES

Just because information is on the web, it does not mean it is true. Anyone can put anything they want on a website. Well-known organisations like the BBC, a university or the Imperial War Museum have sites you can trust. If you are unsure about a site, ask your teacher. Here are a few useful sites to start from (don't forget http:// or http://www.):

angelfire.com/la/raeder/England.html
bbc.co.uk/history/wwtwo.shtml
historyplace.com/worldwar2/timeline/london-blitz.htm
iwm.org.uk/lambeth/lambeth.htm
maelstrom.stjohns.edu/archives/memories.html
members.tripod.com/~Gerry_Wiseman/feature_article.htm

Picture acknowledgements:
The following images courtesy of the Imperial War Museum. Figures following page numbers refer to photograph negative numbers: Cover and imprint page poster: PST0135, cover (centre): HU63751, cover (background): D3167, title page: HU65885, contents page: D3103, p.4: HU5517, p.5 (top): HU36165, (bottom): D1582, p.6 (left): HU36237, (bottom): HU55936, p.7 (top): MH6709, (bottom): HU36238, p.8 (top): 0076, (bottom): MH7545, p.9 (top): HU36248, (centre): HU52714, p.10 (top): D5894, (bottom left): Art Dept poster, (bottom right): S&G30491, p.11 (top) reproduced with the permission of Mrs Jane E. Self, (bottom): HU36217, p.12 (bottom): D2590, p.13 (top): HU59253, (bottom): AP7455B, p.15 (top): HU36195, p.15 (bottom): D17524, p.16 (left): 0137, (bottom): D3097, p.17 (top): D5080, (bottom): D5081, p.18: PL12037, p.19 (top): D2043, p.19 (bottom): D2033, p.20 (top): HU35226, (bottom): D258, p.21 (top): D252, (bottom): D255, p.22 (top): HU36235, (bottom): HU36236, p.23 (top): D3101, (bottom): D3175, p.24 (top left): HU36249, (bottom): HU44273, p.24 (centre): HU36294, p.25 (top right): HU49513, (bottom): D266, p.26 (top): HU36216, p.27: HU36219, p.28: HU36234, p.29 (top): D984, (bottom) HU36233.

Image on p.12 (left) courtesy of Hodder Wayland Picture Library
Image on page 26 (bottom) courtesy of John Frost Newspapers

Map artwork on page 14 by Tim Mayer
Map information and figures taken from Richard Tames, *Life in Wartime Britain*

Sources of quoted material:
Pages 6, 9, 12, 18, 23 (top), 24 and 29 (both): Personal interviews with author
Page 7:   Leonard Smith quote taken from Oonagh Hyndman, ed., *Wartime Kent*, Meresborough Books, Rainham, 1990, p.50
Page 7:   Government announcement taken from *The War Papers*, no.1, Peter Way and Marshall Cavendish Partworks Ltd, London, 1976
Page 8:   Taken from Caroline Lang, *Keep Smiling Through: Women in the Second World War*, CUP, Cambridge, 1989, p.9
Page 10: Taken from Mavis Nicholson, ed., *What Did You Do in the War, Mummy?*, Chatto and Windus, London, 1995, p.19
Page 11: Barbara Letchford quote taken from Oonagh Hyndman, ed., *Wartime Kent*, Meresborough Books, Rainham, 1990, pp.49–50
Page 11: Beryl Cooper quote as above, p.65
Page 13: First two quotes taken from *Ourselves in Wartime*, Odhams, London, p.167
Page 13: Nicola Harrison quote taken from Mavis Nicholson, ed., *What Did You Do in the War, Mummy?*, Chatto and Windus, London, 1995, p.19
Page 17: Lilian Parkes quote taken from Oonagh Hyndman, ed., *Wartime Kent*, Meresborough Books, Rainham, 1990, p.56
Page 17: Anita Bowers quote taken from Caroline Lang, *Keep Smiling Through: Women in the Second World War*, CUP, Cambridge, 1989, p.10
Page 19: Nicola Harrison quote taken from Mavis Nicholson, ed., *What Did You Do in the War, Mummy?*, Chatto and Windus, London, 1995, p.20
Page 19: Lilian Parkes quote taken from Oonagh Hyndman, ed., *Wartime Kent*, Meresborough Books, Rainham, 1990, p.56
Page 21: Pam Hattersley quote taken from Michael Bentinck, ed., *War Time Women*, Michael Bentinck, 1998, p.139
Page 21: Ken Gerring quote taken from Oonagh Hyndman, ed., *Wartime Kent*, Meresborough Books, Rainham, 1990, p.58
Page 23: Quote from evacuee's letter taken from *The War Papers*, no.1, Peter Way and Marshall Cavendish Partworks Ltd., London, 1976
Page 23: Teacher's quote taken from *Ourselves in Wartime*, Odhams, London, p.177
Page 25: Taken from Mavis Nicholson, ed., *What Did You Do in the War, Mummy?*, Chatto and Windus, London, 1995, p.163
Page 28: Taken from Caroline Lang, *Keep Smiling Through: Women in the Second World War*, CUP, Cambridge, 1989, p.7

INDEX

Numbers in **bold** refer to pictures and captions.